QUEUEING FOR THE SUN

Also by U.A. Fanthorpe

Poetry volumes:

Side Effects (Peterloo Poets, 1978)
Standing To (Peterloo Poets, 1982)
Voices Off (Peterloo Poets, 1984)
Selected Poems (Peterloo Poets, 1986, hardcover,
King Penguin, 1986, paperback)
A Watching Brief (Peterloo Poets, 1987)
Neck-Verse (Peterloo Poets, 1992)
Safe as Houses (Peterloo Poets, 1995)
Consequences (Peterloo Poets, 2000)
Christmas Poems (Peterloo Poets & Enitharmon, 2002)

Poetry audio cassettes:

Peterloo Poetry Cassette No. 1(with Elma Mitchell; Peterloo Poets, 1983)
Awkward Subject (Peterloo Poets, 1995)
Double Act (with R.V. Bailey; Penguin audiobook, 1997)

Queueing for the Sun

U.A. FANTHORPE

PETERLOO POETS

First published in 2003
by Peterloo Poets
The Old Chapel, Sand Lane, Calstock, Cornwall PL18 9QX, U.K.

© 2003 by U.A. Fanthorpe

**A catalogue record for this book is available
from the British Library**

ISBN   1-904324-08-8

Printed in Great Britain By
Antony Rowe Ltd, Chippenham, Wilts.

ACKNOWLEDGEMENTS

Acknowledgements and thanks are due to: BBC Radio 3, *Lost London* (Blue Nose Poets), Friends of the Bristol Oncology Centre, *The Guardian*, International Poetry Festival (South Bank), *Mslexia, Poetry Nottingham International, Poetry Review,* The Poetry Proms, *The Reader, Red Wheelbarrow, The Times Literary Supplement, Star Trek – The Poems* (Iron Press), The University of the West of England, and *Waiting Room Poems*.

For Rosie as always

Contents

Queueing for the Sun in Walbrook

(for John Shepherd, and in honour of W F Grimes and A Williams)

The first great London queue.
Not trivial, like the countdown to Harrods sales,
Or charter-flights stacking above Heathrow.
BIG CROWDS AT ROMAN RUIN. MANY
UNABLE TO ENTER. First
Of the serious patient processions: Mithras;
Tutankhamun; Cézanne; Monet.

The only one unearthed in London.
Bull-slayer's temple. His head, with its far-seeing
Merciful eyes, his huge right hand closed on the hilt,
Ready for sacrifice; other bits and pieces,
Gods of all sorts, the usual bones, coins,
Lamps, a hairpin, endless scraps of pots, a candlestick.
MORE FINDS... LATEST FINDS... CHANCE OF MORE DISCOVERIES.

Bombing resurrected the god. A full moon,
Thames at low tide, bringing blitzkrieg
Through the air. Worst raid of the war.
They suffered, Tower, Abbey, Mint,
Westminster Hall, the Commons. London's burning.
But he was still safe, the little foreigner,
DEO INVICTO SOLI MITHRAE
Though Walbrook, Budge Row, Bucklersbury
Fractured on top of him.

After the war, the man,
Grimes, in search of a river. Archaeology,
As usual, against the clock. The builders
Had their blueprints, the developers
Had secured the funding. Some of the unbuilt units

Already let. And Grimes and his little team,
Responsible for all wrecked London, unravelling rubble,
Storing things in paper bags.

On the dig's last day, the god's head,
Decapitated, dirty, alien, moving.
Photographers stalked it, the people came unflagging
To queue, as war had taught them, to see
Something outlandish, risen from London earth,
Wearing their waiting like medals.
CROWDS SEE EIGHTEEN-HUNDRED-YEAR-OLD
ROMAN GOD DUG UP.

The endless orderly march cowed the Cabinet.
Professors wrote letters. Ministers went to see,
Proposed *A week or two more digging?*
His neck materialised. Queues, and more queues,
From Cheapside, the Bank of England, down Walbrook,
Great hungry demonstrations. STILL HOPE
OF REPRIEVE FOR ROMAN TEMPLE.
But of course there wasn't. Money speaks
Louder than Mithras. *I doubt,* said a spokesman,
If this public interest will last.
This is tax-payers' money, after all.

It's still there, and it isn't. Bucklersbury House
Has cornered the holy ground. What you see of the temple,
Re-invented in Queen Victoria Street,
Is in the wrong place, not far enough down,
Looking the wrong way. SOLI INVICTO
AB ORIENTE AD OCCIDENTEM. But the sun
Remains unconquered.

Notes to Queueing for the Sun in Walbrook

Mithras, the god of light and the sun among the Persians, was specially venerated by the Roman army. The Roman temple of Mithras, in the City of London, was probably built AD 240-250; subsequently all traces of it were lost. It began to surface in 1941, during the war, on one of the worst nights of the Blitz. No excavation could be done at that time, but in 1954, which is where the poem begins, the digging was well under way. Professor W F Grimes was in charge of all archaeological excavation in the City. He was in fact tracking the course of the River Walbrook when he came across the temple.

There is a chorus: the headlines of London's evening papers (the *Star, News* and *Standard*); the Latin of the inscriptions; and the voices of civil servants and politicians.

Deo invicto soli Mithrae: to the unconquered sun Mithras
Soli invicto ab oriente ad occidentem: the invincible sun from east to west

The Gaoler's Story

A string of names as long as your arm.
One of those quietish voices, you can tell
He's never had to raise it in his life.

The old school toga, probably descended
From that wolf they all go on about.
Cream de la cream. But I liked him. Really did.

Educated, of course, to the hilt. Only once
I saw him put out. They duffed him up a bit
When they bring him in. He just wiped off the blood –

Knew how to take it. No, but when
He got the message, no more books for him –
Well, then he *was* upset. Covered his head.

I think he was crying. Books, you see, books.
He could face most things with them. Now, take His Kingship
(Theo, we call him, but not to his face),

Brilliant man, brilliant, but books are something
He wouldn't thank you for. Why bother, if you're a king?
Always someone there to read 'em for you

If that's what you want. Bit of a handicap, mind,
For a king not to sign his name. Laws and that
Need signing, He has this gold stencil thing,

And pokes a pen through the holes. Well, it works.
And he's such a superpower he can get away
With murder. Unfortunate phrase. Forget it.

Anyway, make you laugh to see the grandees,
Magisters this and that, Referendariums, Praetorian whatsits
(I don't know what they do) agawp
12

When Theo gets out his stencil and signs
Laws that'll change their lives. And all us Goths
Sniggering up our sleeves. But quietly. He likes us

To get on. Us and the Romans. They're citizens, we're not.
Separate, but equal, says Theo. Well, not quite.
They have the thinking parts, we do the rough.

But yeah, it works. Why, I can't say, unless it's him.
He's strong. Won't take nothing from nobody.
Just as well, with all the gatecrashers we have

Hanging around on the borders. And he minds
About the Stone Age Roman junk. Ruins
That Julius Caesar knocked about a bit

(Or someone). Theatres, walls, drains, aqueducts,
He's seen to 'em all. In Rome and places,
Not just here. You should see the new work in Verona.

Not my cuppa. We're tent-men, as you know.
He's made us comfy here. But there are times
When there's a sort of edginess. This business of B —

I don't want to talk about it. But I wasn't happy,
The sort of man B was, things that went on.
My hands are clean. But whether that's enough

I'll never know. Could I have done something
More than I did to help? He was good to me,
He spared me pain. Odd for a gaolbird

To do that for a gaoler, but he did.

You have to understand, there's always been
This wild streak in His Kingship. Not battle-wildness —
That's reasonable. But stabbing a man at a feast

13

(Twice he's done that) when peace is declared and all.
Had the bodyguard eliminated, killed the brother,
Wife locked up (she died of hunger), kids

Eradicated. For some it's a way of life,
But not for him. Just blows a gasket sometimes.
Daresay he had to do it. We mightn't be here

If he hadn't. And really he's civilized
In the Roman way, apart from not reading and writing,
And these little accidents.

       civilised accidents
  see   what happened
                    I don't want
    it isn't easy

B was the one who knew about everything:
Music, the stars, the gods, philosophy
(His word. He taught me it. I didn't know it),

Poetry (he wrote it), logic (never grasped that),
Sums of all sorts, how to make clocks,
Not a thing but he understood its workings.

It's curtains for our world, he'd say to me,
I'm saving what I can, to smuggle through the darkness,
So people after'll know about Plato and Arry

(Two Greek geezers. He'd translated them before.
He thought the world of them. He put them in Latin,
In case Greek didn't last. Languages don't, he said.).

In prison, of course, he hadn't got his books,
All that, *finito*. He started a new thing
(A man you couldn't stop), called Consolation.

Now that's a queer thing. Who'd console you,
In jug, everything lost, disgraced? Wife, child, maybe,
But for him it was this philosophy, a high-class dame

Who ticks him off for being in the blues,
For listening to Poetry and all that stuff
(*Shop-soiled tarts* she called them) and tells him

Listen to her and *she'll* make him
Snap out of it. So she does. All rather above my head,
But she does. And then he couldn't finish it.

He knew what was coming. How, I don't know.
One morning gave me what he had, and the papers
(*Hand 'em to the future,* he said. The old joke),

And put through his last request to Theo. Wouldn't say
What it was. I supposed wife, kids, as aforesaid.
But it wasn't that. It was me. He wanted me out

When it came to doing him in. Thinking it over after,
I guess he knew I couldn't take it. Not enough Philosophy.
And he was right. I think he liked me. Even, in a way, loved.

He knew so much, he saw so much. He was rare.
I still can't bear it. Couldn't have borne to see
The executioners coming in. The way they did it,

Cords twisted round his head, and jerked
Until his eyes came out. Then clubbed to death.
He saved me this, and died his beastly death

Alone, as in a way he always was. With Plato,
And Arry, and Philosophy.

                    When I go out
And see the stars at night, I think of him.

15

Notes *These notes are for those who like notes. Please don't feel you have to read them.*

The events took place at the beginning of mediaeval history. The last Roman Emperor of the West (Romulus) was deposed in 476AD. Theodoric was born in c.454, Boethius in c.480.

Theodoric ruled the Western Empire from Ravenna, having led the Ostrogoths into Italy. They didn't count as Roman citizens, and Theodoric himself didn't claim the title of Imperator; he was officially a sort of viceroy, using the title *Rex*. He allowed his Goths one third of his lands; the Romans had the rest. The Goths retained their own laws and customs, but Theodoric followed the Roman administrative system and used officials trained in the Imperial services. He was a great restorer of Roman remains. His achievement in reconciling Romans and Goths was amazing, but there were occasional outbursts of ferocity on his part. He ruled Italy for thirty years, dying in 526AD.

B: Anicius Manlius Severinus Boethius (c.480-524AD). Roman scholar, philosopher, statesman. Consul in 510 under King Theodoric. Eventually Boethius lost favour, was accused of treason and magic, and was executed. He wrote his great work *De Consolatione Philosophiae* while in prison in Tichenum (now Pavia), waiting for death. He wanted to translate the whole of Aristotle's works and Plato's *Dialogues* into Latin, and explain them – a life's work. He failed in this, but what he did translate was vital; only through Boethius's translation of *Logic* did knowledge of Aristotle survive in the west, and his work made the whole of mediaeval (and subsequent) learning possible. That *De Consolatione Philosophiae* was translated into English by King Alfred, Chaucer and Queen Elizabeth gives some indication of its importance.

B's Translations: Knowledge of the Greek language was dying out in the West, hence Boethius's hurry to translate Greek thought into Latin. He correctly anticipated centuries of ignorance in the future, and wanted to make sure the best things lasted.

Plato and Arry: Plato and Aristotle

Morning After

The bass, crowing voices of women
Who have cried all night. Men blowing vengeance
Sulkily into their moustaches. The legions
Keeping an eye on the natives, of course,
But rather huffed about demarcation rights,
Drily comparing blisters. And himself,
Aloofly ticking off another milestone
On immortality's Roman Road.

And the wood not a wood at all,
But a mouth after extraction. The oozing
Stumps, the pale grass which had never
Seen daylight, the smashed long bodies
Of trees. Proper woodcutters work primly,
Leave clean piles of timber behind them, delight
In bunches of kindling, the smell of resin,
Know the uses of bark. This wood was holy,
So it was butchered by frightened soldiers.
Sacred birds and severed heads had nested
In its hollow places. Now strange creakings
Happened, strange pools opened, and strange
Wicked smells. Lumps underfoot
Were sometimes only dead birds, and sometimes
Something nastier. There was space of a kind
Where had always been trees. Even the sky
Looked surprised and odd, as if no one
Had seen that piece before.

You can't blame Caesar. Being
A top Roman, he naturally did
The Roman thing. Trees aren't citizens,
At least, not this sort, only
The tapering ones with classical profiles.
These were undisciplined, scattering

Acorns and magic with barbarian
Abandon. Also they lacked *gravitas*,
Or perhaps they had too much
Of the wrong sort. Anyway, Caesar
Gave them the chop. The soldiers
Were hanging fire, discussing hylophobia's
Fancier symptoms, so he made the first
Nick himself, yelling *OK chaps,*
Me for scapegoat. Now take your
*Fingers out.**

What had he done? He didn't
Wait to find out. Being, as usual,
In a hurry to get on, *dux tamen impatiens,*
He was off to Spain while oaks, yews, alders
Were still toppling. Don't, by the way, suppose
He had the wood down for reasons
Of superstition. The only magic he believed in
Was his own luck. He just needed planks
For beseiging Marseilles, and these were handy.

But the wood caught up with him; woods do.
He died with naked swords in his face,
Like a wild beast taken by hunters,
Among the Senate-house's marble pillars.

* *Iam ne quis vestrum dubitet subvertere silvam,*
Credite me fecisse nefas.

Lucan, *The Civil War, III 436-7*

At Gunthorp, November 2000

(The defeat of the Roman IX Legion by Boudicca's forces may have taken place at
Gunthorp)

Once it was after the battle. The beaten
Lay choked in their litter.

Now is after the storms. The weir groans
Like all-night city traffic.

The next field in, said the dog-walker.
Unless it's the kingfisher you're after.
He's based by the sluice.

Plastic, shattered branches,
Rags, paper, binliners,
Dislodged from their lurking places,
Muffle the staggering bushes,

Like the fallout after battle,
Like the Ninth when it was over.

Fields seems to be river, and
The unbanked river has
Lost patience with its own logic.

It was the herons we were after,
And there they were, in the lee of the hedge,
Hunched, patient, deadly.
Their killer's beaks. Their raucous shouts
Echoing after.

Sprung

Acts 12:3-11

Imprisoned for the third time, knowing
Death is tomorrow. You get used to these things.
There have been my shameful sleeps
In the past. So now, shackled between
Two monstrous guards, squads at all doors
Throughout the prison, I said my prayers:
To Him, and Him my friend, then nodded off.
You'd sleep through Armageddon
My mother used to say.

A ghastly dream: cocks crowing round me;
A man called Malchus showing me his ear;
I never met the man; fall into fishy water;
Cocks, *Never!* ears, water. Me asleep.

Something rather like a prod woke me.
I sat up. The guards snored on. Even
The ones at the doors had their heads down.
Light blinked from nowhere. My chains fell off,
Left blackened scars behind. A hint, a hint
From somewhere. *Must get going.* Almost I heard
Someone say *Clothes! shoes! coat!* but no one
Was there, just me doing these things,
All thumbs.
         I didn't know my way down
The prison corridors, but my way found me.
Guards motionless (drunk to the world, no doubt).
Still I moved dimly, a man in a dream,
As far as the vast impenetrable gates.

Now I could smell sweet freedom's city smells,
Dust, fishheads, carrion, shit, muck, man,
Felt the city wind blowing on my cheek.

                                        No exit.
Nothing could get past *them*. Might as well
Go back to my chains.
                        Hard to explain.
But as I stood, the gates, the impenetrable gates,
Opened themselves to me. Gracious, as if I were
A lord coming home. It seemed a dream still, but
It wasn't. There was wet on the ground, from
Yesterday's rain. A voice I knew (it seemed like His voice)
Seemed to say *Follow me*. So I walked through
The mannerly gates, into the street.
                                        Someone was with me.
Had he been there all the time? *He* thought he had.
Hugging me round the shoulders (and I hugged him),
Saying *We've done it, Pete!* and – hey presto! – vanished.
Me, looking up and down and sideways after him,
And just a clutch of feathers in my fist.

The Obituarists

The genealogist is meticulous.
He harries his subject back to Adam
(Forty-two generations–if you can believe that.)

Scene 1: the playwright's way in,
Smack in the middle of a river.
Enter a man wearing camel's hair,
Chewing insects.

The novelist deploys more characters
Than Cecil B de Mille: shepherds, angels,
Emperors, wizards, mother (a mute).
He keeps the hero up his sleeve till later.

Babies, bit players, aren't part
Of the mystic's agenda. He starts with aplomb
And a metaphor.

The subject himself: a man not much given
To writing things down. Once
He scraped a message on the ground with a finger.
No one seems to have noticed.
If they did, it was soon scuffed out.

The Dagda

The Celts had a god for it.
Not the handsome sort, with a sportsman's torso,
Manhandling thunder or laurels,

Not arachnoid Indian,
With too many legs for comfort, nor austere
Egyptian, with an ibis's

Profile. A do-it-yourself
God, with artisan's thumbs, and screws, twine, wrenches,
Glue, stuffed in his poacher's pockets.

In sweaty working-clothes, hard
And unbeautiful, shouldering his crude club,
He stands, looking around for work.

Who would employ such a tough?
The gods only know he brews in his homely
Kitchen the recipe of life.

Autumn Double

CELTIC FEAST

This is the day which is no day,
Belonging neither with what has been
Nor with what is to be.

This is the day which is not,
When the other people come
From the other kingdom,

Missing the boundaries between
Their kingdom and ours, for this is the day
When there are no boundaries.

Tomorrow we shall do many things.
We shall slaughter the cattle, we shall celebrate
The coming together of the goddess and the god.

We shall eat pork, to each
His appropriate portion. The leg for the king,
The haunch for the queen, the head for the charioteer.

For the hero, the whole porker.
We shall drink wine tomorrow, and sacrifice.
There will be races. We shall applaud the bards.

Tomorrow we shall do these things
Which are required of us. Today
Is a day not ours. We do nothing in it

But wait and fear. This is the day
When trees and earth speak in one language,
Being all the colour of fire.

This is the day when the other people
Drift over our boundaries like fog.
We have no power against them

And the doomed cattle are starved, and bawl,
Distressing the children. And the day is short,
Even on high ground. And we are unprotected.

BONFIRE NIGHT

We are the other people.
Do our random fires puzzle your night?
Do you seek a word of power to halt
The hornless beasts with golden eyes
That trample our drove-ways?

Our ghost-fires burn
In the wrong places, on low ground,
In gardens. Their reek disturbs
Like a bruised memory. We have lost
The peaceful dialectic of Samain.

We are the other people.
Your seers glimpse our dwarf priests
As on low carts they trundle
The blank-faced god down stone paths.
You are right to be scared of our kingdom.

Driving South

Nothing will happen to us all the way.
Counties drop back, known only to our tyres.
The dog sleeps in the back. The engine purrs.
Sun, trees and cooling towers become a dream,
A world we pass through, never see.

A sudden shriek knifes our tranquillity.
Have we run down a rabbit, killed a bird?
Nothing so harmless. We have passed by Towton.
What's done is quivering here, alive and dying.

The bloody names pursue. York, Selby, Richmond,
Pomfret, where Richard died. History hounds us.
The sign posts stretch like hands, bonefingered, endless,
Pointing us to a sorrow we can't share,
Scorning our ignorance, compelling knowledge.

Here battle was. Here the king bled to death,
The martyr hung in chains. And once we know
The grand, heraldic cruelties, we sense
Enormous suffering behind each hedge.
Here a whole village was wiped out, and here
Hundreds of peasants slowly starved to death.

We break into the present when we stop
For petrol. But the past intrudes here too.
The man who serves us wears the same grim sign.
Has a child died, or is his wife unfaithful?
At least in his case we aren't forced to know.

Suffering riddles England. Rubbish bins
Are not enough for even our modest present;
How can they hold the litter of the past?

The Vulgar Tongue

I am old, weatherbeaten, subtle.
Invasion and invention have taught me
Not to be surprised by anything.

One of nature's lifeboats, I survive
Instinctively, out of habit. Sidelong
I am aware of foundering craft,

Sanskrit, Esperanto, Manx. Something
Intransigent in their rig makes them apt
To capsize. I, on the other hand,

Like a prostitute, accommodate
Anything at all. To be alive is
What counts. My mystery persists for

Babies and poets to juggle with
In this dead landscape. And when they touch me,
I go off like a bomb.

Caedmon's song

Forst ther wes nowt nowt and neewhere
God felt the empty space wi his finga
Let's hev sum light sez God
Ootbye and inbye so the light happened.

Up ower theer, thowt God, airy and open
We'll hev a sky and a shavin' of cloud
Here's a bit watter we'll caal this whale-road
Dolphin-drive, duck alley Davey Jones' locka.

Next orth appeared a canny bit greenstuff
Rhubarb an raspberry leafcome an leaf-faal.

God saw the heavens wes handsome but homely
Made sun and moon an the sharp stars their marrers.
Gannen to be good, sez God, else Ah'm a gowk.

Friday he thowt on flatfish an flounders
Halibut, hake an haddock an herrin
Likewise the cushat chunterin an clockin
Seagull an skylark an the shrewd spuggy.

Last cam the fowk, so canny an careful
Hey, bonny lads, sez God, how will this suit yez?

The version of Caedmon's Hymn we are all familiar with is from Bede's Latin, usually
rendered in a Whitby voice. There is also a rather longer and more detailed MS in
Northumbrian OE, here presented as the modern Tyneside idiom.

(J G Collingwood, *The Harp Refused: Caedmon and his Hymn*)

Jonson at Hawthornden

(Drummond speaks)

He must have left a lick of himself behind,
After that famous twenty-stone trudge from London.

Endless infallible views of the man who knows
All about everything (most of it damaging):

Shakespeare lacked art; Sidney was plain; Petrarch
A blackguard for over-production of sonnets.

I wasn't exactly unnerved. But he kept on.
He'd killed his two men, twice done time in the Clink –

There's a clutch of eminent mortal enemies after him.
He'll write, he says, about his visit here.

He calls himself The Poet. I'm
Too good and simple, it seems. Would

Be wise to give up on poetry. Won't excel.
And yet this bin of flesh, this brawling bully

Writes O such sweet and O such tender verse.
He is the nonpareil he says he is.

But God be praised, he's gone. I'll write my comment
(A great lover and praiser of himself)

Then pace my paths, and listen to my rooks.
Rude swaggerers, they have a touch of him.

(Jonson came to Hawthornden in the summer of 1618, and seems to have left early in
January 1619. See the enormously entertaining *Conversations*, noted down by Drummond,
who says nothing at all himself. All this is in *Ben Jonson*, ed. Ian Donaldson, OUP, 1985.)

The Man Who Loved Gardens

Being a gentleman
Of parts, he knew the parts
He played included Adam,
Eve, serpent and fiery angel.

He was Adam the mower
With a democratic passion
For grass, and an unhandy
Knack of nicking his own ankle.

Eve, he fancied, had been
Maligned. Sagely he loved
Plain, noble, pre-pubescent
Little girls, grew his hair, never married
But mastered the definition of love.

As for the serpent, being
Beautiful and equivocal, not
To mention belonging in a garden,
He couldn't resist it.

Cagey reporting of parliamentary
Business to the watery borough
That drowned his father
Barred him from other men's Edens,

So he presided with irony
Over sublunary confusions,
Reconciling the irreconcilable
Nature of things with a pun.

Hardy Country

(for Nancy Williams)

Being himself deciduous, he knew
The sadness of the fall of the leaf,
Was moved by the staring heads
Of trucked cattle on their way
To slaughter, suffered all his life
From the fieldfare his father killed
By mistake one bad winter.
A name changed on a Dorchester
Shopfront subdued him. In old age
He avoided his parents' senile
Bockhampton house,
Being himself deciduous.

Being mortal ourselves, we wince
As his leaves go down. We mark
The Americans at the bottom
Of his parents' garden drinking wine
From plastic cups. We estimate
The impossibility of a party
In the shrunken livingroom. We observe
The unimportant letters framed,
And a headscarfed Caucasian Tess
With moody translated eyes
Somehow inching away from Marlott,
Being mortal ourselves.

What was never true is always
Truer than truth. *The Forestry Commission*
Has made quite a difference to Egdon,
But still the path from Puddletown
Greenly unreels, and the young trim man
Steps down it briskly to found
His Dorset dynasty. Cream teas

And juggernaut lorries preside
In Casterbridge, but still the broody Mayor
Paces its littered pavements. Heartless at Stinsford,
Tucked between Florence Emily and Emma Lavinia,
Be comforted, old man. The tree's still growing.

On the Wing

(for Anne Stevenson)

Obedient to some private calendar
She comes, stays, goes. She knows the others,
The ocean-airborne from Siberia to Severn;
Small brown birds nipping down homely hedgerows;
On-the-wing swifts like cut air falling in shrieks...

> *Right. Yes. Hang on.*
> *Is she a bird, your poet?*

In some ways, yes. She soars from state to state,
Grounding, leaving a private sign of love,
Her signature, a poem of the place,
In Hay-on-Wye, Oxford, Vermont,
Michigan, Cambridge, Durham...

> *Ah.*
> *Some sort of migrant?*

Mostly you'll find her silent, spellbound. She broods
On everyday things, has time for unorthodox weeds
That farmers damn: Himalayan Balsam,
Ragwort – of course, they're migrants, too...

> *Just a sec.*
> *What about us, the stay-at-homes?*

O she watches the small kempt gardens of Cambridge,
Its cold mercenary bathrooms, the educated earth
Of Oxford. Watches them like a lover,
And the lives inside, around. Remembers
Insignificant people doing insignificant things
Knows the idiom of children, and of cats...

Sounds nice.
Where could I find her?
In cities, and countries, in the weather,
Passing through, whenever there's life,
There, watching it, attentive...

But I'm still confused.
Is she a bird or a poet?

Ah, that's the interesting thing...

n.b. All the best lines and words in this poem have been pilfered from A.S.

Probably unique in this state

(for Peter Scupham)

I've been stupid, shape-changer.
You scattered the clues to your selves
So wittily that all the cul-de-sacs
Shimmer like nighttime motorways,
While motorways dwindle into dead ends.

But now I've rumbled you, shape-changer
(Your passion for Shakespeare gives you away),
You are Puck, the pwca, pooke, poakes
(I mention this to please your bookishness).

Puck who knows woodlands, feels for elms,
Visits the Underground, hears the sea-maid's music,
Has a taste for acting, interferes with sadness,
Has a special relish for transformation,

Who magics tired discarded books
Into volumes of delight, rescues
A *cock-eyed* house (no doubt it needed magic)
Just the place for *a play to be toward.*

Above all poet who acknowledges
Old forgotten things, the whimpering dead,
Who tracks them down and gives them voices,
Resurrects them with his words.

Lover of slim folios and stout volumes,
Discoverer of *1300 vivacious pages,*
Mint yourself, though maybe *rather used,*
You who promise us *No Deep Confessions,*
Football, Sustained Philosophical Thought,
Enmities, or Poems About Dogs.

You who hear, before us mortals,
The morning lark, who follow darkness
Like a dream, you with your flair
For the preposterous, you to whom Shakespeare
Gives the last word, the Epilogue,

Mandeville, Mermaid, Peter, Puck,
This comes with love, and brings good luck.

Poet at the Festival

('... school parties welcome...')

Not just the lunchtime regulars with *Guardians*,
Handbags, scarves and coughs.
The hall's packed, and half of it has bare knees
And PE next.

(In Thrace they knew what to do
With dangerous folk like you:
Tore 'em in two.)

Some of it lolls legless
In wheelchairs, wades in
On angled feet. The palsied,
The maimed young; and the adults, hale.

They think he's *bonkers*.

Only you, Sir,
Knew what to do
With this bunch. *Right!*
Who's eleven? And hands sprout.

He's used to the cross-legged
Who call him *Sir*. He knows they'll come,
The mad treble giggles,
When he says *bra* or *bum*.

He has a word from the holy mountain,
And a word for the titterers.
He will say both words.

(In Thrace they knew what to do.)

He shows us how to laugh at him
Participation time!
For being Gulliver, for being *bonkers*.

He doesn't laugh at us.
He has spoken both words,
And we have understood one of them.

He has been to the holy mountain in Thrace,
And has come back in two pieces.
He has given us his two pieces.
Laughing, we take them.

Bless us, Sir.

Harried

They can't ignore it. Larkin in libraries,
Wordsworth in Westmorland, up to the eyes
In stamps, Yeats being senatorial,
Burns fixing taxes, Milton rubbing up
Latin shorthand, Chaucer hard at work
Controlling customs, Wools, Skins and Tanned Hides
(Which must have kept him busy), Marvell hoping
His interest in Hull wouldn't dissolve
Before Parliament did, sad crazy Clare,
Whose plough made crazy furrows in the sad
Northampton earth, and Mr Eliot,
Fault-finding in Lloyd's ledgers, most of all
Shakespeare, enduring conferences with Burbage,
Explaining why he couldn't make the part
Of Hamlet longer, all the time unwritten sonnets
Trickling out of his fingers' ends and running
To waste on the sandy floor. I see them all
Turning an honest penny, perpetually
Worrying that their best thoughts coincided
With a perforation problem, or Cromwell
Declaring war on the Scots. How much better
Poets or employees they would have been,
If they had turned their backs on poetry
Or work. Work doesn't mind. But poetry
Wouldn't leave them alone.

Entertaining Poets

One of them was sulky
And would speak only
Welsh. One of them had just
Left prison (a sexual
Offence), and one was
Resting between nervous
Breakdowns, and must not be
On her own, ever,
Or she would destroy herself.
One ate, with a passionate
Angry absorption, everything
Available, and cast
Covetous eyes at other
People's plates. One seemed
Unremarkable at the time
But bombarded us later
With remaindered slim
Volumes and obese bills.

It seems wrong to comment
On their difference
From us. After all, they
Did their best to seem the same,
Never mentioned bay
Leaves or inspiration,
But concentrated on
Sales and technique like
Any solid citizen
Who knows how it's done, and is
Willing for a small fee to
Demonstrate unimportant trade
Secrets. Kinder on the
Whole to be fooled by their

Camouflage, pretend
These are our equals, not creatures
Helplessly wired to the wrong
End of the Muse's one-way telephone line.

Workshop's End

True happiness consists not in a multitude of friends,
but in their worth and choice.   (Dr Johnson)

In the old stories, when the band
At last dissolves, they go their separate ways,
Robin, the Friar, Maid Marian and the rest,
The merry men. I'm desolate.
I want them all to stay together,
Whatever the weather,
For ever.

I know they can't. They've other lives to lead,
Must marry, emigrate, turn respectable,
But in my head they're still walking the greenwood
Together, for ever. The last pages
Are never opened.

Now, our last page. Year by year we've walked
The enchanted workshop ground: the dark magician;
The Yorkshire truth-teller; the humble one
Who thought she couldn't do it; me. We have explored
Bravely, in difficult places. We've laughed a lot.
We've loved, not thinking much about it.
We've stayed together,
We thought, for ever.

Now no more. Well, things do end,
However much I like to think they don't.
But we shall keep this rare and sideways knowledge
Of you, of you, of you and me,
Effect of workshop camaraderie
Together. In these poems,
Whatever the weather,
It lasts for ever.

Secret Garden

There's no such thing. Gardens are never secret.
If a single swan (as here) complacently
Inverts itself on a lake, then at once another
Shows up, thrumming its way through air. One human
(As here) in a garden means another somewhere,
Categorizing umbelliferae,
Transmitting a therapeutic kiss, or in search of a cutting.

Then there's the infiltrators. Artists omit them.
But consider the endlessness of worms, the manic
Engineering of moles. Serpents, of course,
Famously get into gardens. And if the painter
Had more room for sky, there'd surely have been
Some gull drifting over, taking a bird's eye view.

The genuine secret garden is suburban,
A couple of cupfuls of sour clay, wrenched
From railway embankments and ring-roads,
Where every grass-blade's cut by hand. No robin ventures
For fear of leaving a claw-mark.

However high their walls, all gardens
Are open cities. And, as astronauts know,
All the world's a garden. All the men
And women jobbing gardeners, discouraging green.

Leave any tarmacked scrap for a moment, and something
Comes quietly through: ivy, grass, bramble,
The great first-footers. Other feet, too.
A fox may winter out in that potting shed,
And lovers know how to climb over orchard walls.
As, if she's lucky, here.

Route des Grappes

Here come the young ones,
The green boys, the dancers.

In spring each coltish shoot
Makes every way a bright gamble.

In summer, tendril by tendril,
They beat the bounds of their domain.

In autumn, dense with cropping,
Gravely they finish the pace
Of the green men's measure.

In other countries, other years,
Drinkers will taste the skin
Of these dancing feet, and music
From the land of green boys will pierce
Expense-account-lunch-flushed
Ears, gorged eyes will grow tender,
As with their rash vines the green ones lasso
The knives and forks, the salt, the clever dealers.

Marriage Lines

Being silent (even her postcards
Were curter that other people's),
She inclined to the company
Of the more reserved plants

Gardens are safer than men to love.
They betray naturally and
Helplessly. No one expects
A garden to be faithful.

So she reverted to grass. The stone
Bowls brimmed, the fruit trees' branches bore
Down on the daisies. Nothing much
Was ever pruned or stopped.

The garden grew into the house. Lawns,
Beds and pools amalgamated.
Only robins obstinately
Stayed territorial.

And he, feeling no fellowship with
Hedges, strayed like honeysuckle
Over other mens' smart borders,
Sowing seeds of children.

The Beasts

After the flood, they left the Ark.
(Two by two, Hurrah Hurrah Hurrah)
Noah had saved them. Life was good.
(All together now. Hurrah Hurrah).

Noah had a vision of his sons
(One and two and three. Hurrah Hurrah)
A vision of fur and tusks and skins,
Of rifles, poison, harpoons, gins,
A whiff of battery hens (Hurrah Hurrah),

Draize-tested rabbits, cattle trucks,
(Thousands and thousands. Money for us. Hurrah)
Myxomatosis and abattoirs,
The pheasant shoot, the *corrida*
(Money and death. Hurrah Hurrah Hurrah).

Noah remembered the forty days
(The Arkful of precious lives. Hurrah Hurrah)
Tiger, panda, bittern, cod,
He knew how dear they were to God
(Who made them all. Hurrah Hurrah Hurrah).

He knelt down so the worms could hear
(No one counts worms. Hurrah Hurrah Hurrah)
He said, *You creatures great and small,*
My sons will soon destroy you all.
Scram! But they didn't scram nearly far
Enough
      (Hurrah
          Hurrah)

Herons

Trappists, reciting each his
Solitary office from
A damp station;

Executioners,
Patient and precise as death, axing
The lay gudgeon;

Black-queued mandarins, sloping
Off in a bundle of long
Bones, huffily

Assaulting airways to your
High-rise slums, where you turn
Starling vulgar

Commuters from the M6,
Family men and harassed
Mothers of five

On a limited budget,
With House of Commons manners;

Remote celibate in the
Grey and white of your order,
Fisher of fish,

Or parent, slave to instinct
And procreation; are you
Such artists at

Living that both your selves can
Co-exist comfortably
Uncompromised?

Caravan

(for Eddie)

Garden grandees, they mince along the way.
Their trains glisten. Black and gold their flags,
Solemn their pacing.

> *Ah! the men and boys, the torches and the singing,*
> *Camels sure-footed in the grey sand of morning.*

The straining feet, the heavy precious bales,
The antlered crowns depressed in holy thought,
Sombre their purpose.

> *Ah! the last of the town-walls, as the dusty cloud*
> *Crawls in the mid-day desert. And the singing.*

Ah! the fair green flesh of the predestined
Young helpless dahlias.

The Apple War

The storm troops have landed,
The red and the green,
Their pips on their shoulders,
Their skin brilliantine.

Uniform, orderly,
Saleable, ambitious –
Gala and Granny
And Golden Delicious.

Quarter them, they're tasteless;
They've cotton-wool juice,
But battalions of thousands
Routinely seduce.

In shy hen-haunted orchards
Twigs faintly drum,
Patient as partisans
Whose time has almost come,

From Worcester and Somerset,
Sussex and Kent,
They'll ramble singing,
A fruity regiment.

Down with Cinderella's kind,
Perfect toxic, scarlet;
Back comes the old guard
Costard, Crispin, Russet.

James Grieve, Ashmead Kernel,
Coppin, Kingston Black –
Someone has protected them.
They're coming back.
50

West Bay in Winter

Landscape of absentees, where nothing
Is in itself, but anticipates
Patiently the next coming.

Landscape of withdrawn teashops, of shut
Pizzerias and doughnutteries,
Lavatories out of order.

Brooding self-absorbed till Easter makes
Sense of immense carparks, hides duckboards
And sandbags for a season.

Showers chase us, and mysterious light
Behind clouds falls on water we can't
Quite see. Gulls alone mark us.

Caravans turn their backs like cattle.
Laked fields lie apathetic. Only
The sea, that old ham, relentlessly
Goes on performing.

Wotton Walks

These are old paths, designed
And kept alive by feet
For whom walking was
The only way of going.

These are treads of workers,
Plodding early with their bait
To quarries, mills, farms; haunts
Of fishermen; rides for fine
Ladies, cantering sidesaddle
Through polished woodland; sly poaching alleys;
Game-keepers' beats; loitering ways for children
Towards ball-games and arithmetic; paths
For dutiful daughters to mothers'
Picturesque rheumaticky cottages;
By-ways for primrose-finders; the straight gate
To church for tidy-suited hymn-singers;
Trails for dog-tired shepherds to remote
Huts at lamb-time; muddy channels
For heavy patient cows; close turf
And easy gravel for foxes and badgers
To travel after dark.
                    Enter this web
Spun by dead and living round Wotton.
Remember lovers keeping trysts
At special stiles, remember
Gipsies stealing down green lanes,
And the reflective fellows
Who watched and thought by bridges
Over small streams. Attend also
To the punctually returning
Tree, flower, bird, since what you see
Is as new as it's old.
                    Finally,

Come back satisfied, please, at peace,
To where Wotton pleats herself on her shelves
Above the vale, under the edge.

Extras

Two of them, always.
That is part of the story.

Speech, and Silence. The wit,
Who chats up soldiers, speaks the epitaph,
Who knows the score,

And Iras, golden-mouthed,
Says less than Cordelia, even.

There is a soothsayer, to amuse
The women. But she is the one who knows,

Her words being dragged from the future
Into now. One dies before, one after.

The fig-seller's snake articulates them both,
But Iras goes first, dying of a queen's kiss;

Charmian later, contradicting a Roman.

The usual things are happening to the world:
Battles on land, battles at sea, pacts, violations of pacts,

Empire-building, empire-losing, men jobbing, men getting
On with the job, eagles, pyramids, yarns about wives and crocodiles.

In the dangerous centre of the court,
Eunuchs, messengers, decisions, jokes,

And the two, always,
One before, one after,
Who do nothing but die,
Being part of the story.

Administrator

Underling too long, though finally you made it
To top dog, you knew the system too well
To bark authentically.

You, the expert on short cuts, on first-name terms
With the influential – stores, post-room, porters; you
Who knew how to fix it,

Whose good deeds were always shady, like
The fiddled day off for Christmas shopping, which
Was rightfully ours;

You who scrounged, never spent, who shook
With fright before committees, who always forgot
Your own authority;

Who dared not sanction our electric kettles,
Whose kindnesses were home-made, compensation
For your servile failure
To improve anything.

A Minor Role

I'm best observed on stage,
Propping a spear, or making endless
Exits and entrances with my servant's patter,
Yes, sir. O no, sir. If I get
These midget moments wrong, the monstrous fabric
Shrinks to unwanted sniggers.

But my heart's in the unobtrusive,
The waiting-room roles: driving to hospitals,
Parking at hospitals. Holding hands under
Veteran magazines; making sense
Of consultants' monologues; asking pointed
Questions politely; checking dosages,
Dates; getting on terms with receptionists;
Sustaining the background music of civility.

At home in the street you may see me
Walking fast in case anyone stops:
O, getting on, getting better my formula
For well-meant intrusiveness.
                                    At home,
Thinking ahead: *Bed? A good idea!*
(Bed solves a lot); answer the phone,
Be wary what I say to it, but grateful always;
Contrive meals for a hunger-striker; track down
Whimsical soft-centred happy-all-the-way-through novels;
Find the cat (mysteriously reassuring);
Cancel things, tidy things; pretend all's well,
Admit it's not.

Learn to conjugate all the genres of misery:
Tears, torpor, boredom, lassitude, yearnings

For a simpler illness, like a broken leg.

Enduring ceremonial delays. Being referred
Somewhere else. Consultant's holiday. Saying *Thank you*
For anything to everyone.
                              Not the star part,
And who would want it? I jettison the spear,
The servant's tray, the terrible drone of Chorus:
Yet to my thinking this act was ill-advised
*It would have been better to die**. No, it wouldn't!

I am here to make you believe in life.

*Chorus: from *Oedipus Rex*, trans. E F Watling

Waiting Room

I am the room for all seasons,
The waiting room. Here the impatient
Fidget, gossip, yawn and fret and sneeze. I am the room

For summer (sunburn, hay-fever, ear wax,
Children falling out of plum trees, needing patching);

For autumn (arthritis and chesty coughs,
When the old feel time worrying at their bones);

For winter (flu, and festival hangovers,
Flourish of signatures on skiers' plaster of Paris);

For spring (O the spots of adolescence,
Unwary pregnancies, depression, various kinds of itch):

I am the room that understands waiting,
With my box of elderly toys, my dog-eared *Woman's Owns*,
Permanent as repeat prescriptions, unanswerable as ageing,
Heartening as the people who walk out smiling, weary

As doctors and nurses working on and on

A Brief Resumé at Fifty

Now, let's have a brief resumé.
Ah that's better. (The Goons)

November. The clocks go back and the lights come on.
In a fall of paper flowers we remember the dead.

Born after Remembrance, in start-again November,
When brooks run high, and Wales is clear over Severn,
When raindrops juggle on fences in early mornings,
And wild swans are drumming their way back to Slimbridge,

Born in the pinched post-war, when, cold and discouraged,
We had too much to remember, too many uncounted deaths,
You came, a wordless message, bringing the future with you,
Into a past-haunted world.

Babies are famous for doing this. But royal babies
Trail our history along with theirs.
At your grandfather's great-grandmother's jubilee, my grandfather
Held up my baby father to see. His first memory

Of anything. Sir, you are past and future, Cerdic of Wessex
And CD Rom. It all comes together in you,

The focus, the pioneer, the first to be born
With a zoom lens in your face. For you the usual
Confusions of childhood were public; for you
Adolescent pratfalls were headlines; for you marriage

A monstrously slow-motion fuss, viewed raptly worldwide,
Which every citizen could recite by heart, errata included.
And then the fairytale death
Of the sad and lovely; and the tongue-tied people,
The angry eloquence of flowers all over the island,
The dogged unweeping slow march behind the coffin.

59

These things happen to us all, or most of them do,
Only no one bothers to look. (*Zoom*, says the lens.)
Now, for your fiftieth birthday, we wish you
A happier landfall,
A *Now* when the worst things are over, or at least
One knows how to handle them. Not the start of life,
But the start of freedom, of *looking*
(As Shakespeare grandly says) *with such large discourse,*
Before and after.

When you came we were looking backwards. Now
There's the future to see to.
Where you're standing means a lot of going:
Kalahari, Canada, the Caribbean, meeting
Generals, philosophers, artists, people,
Always people, in the rainy streets,
With their handshakes, their flags, their flowers.

And the quiet places, where protocol is different,
Where a kilt is possible and children are safe;
The modest undistinguished bit of Gloucestershire,
Old Shallow's country; all of it,
This fragile special island, mauled by the sea,
Frittered away by speculators, eaten
By money-grubbers. Yours, Sir, by inheritance
To care for.
                    With that well-known polite
Diffidence to all comers.

                    It's your birthday.
May the enterprises thrive; may buildings
Be humane and gracious; may broadcasters and writers
Deal fairly with English; may the unemployed
Get work worth doing; may the Duchy
And all its doings flourish; may

Your Gloucestershire garden grow.

Lying on paths and grass the dead flat leaves;
Jutting already on branches, next year's buds.

For Sophie and Margaret

(and for Jane Healy and Gillian Forshaw, who helped me write it)

It snowed overnight, Sophie,
And someone (a shy admirer? your lover?)
Wrote s o p h i e in careful Marion Richardson
Outside my kitchen window in the snow.

I walked round your name in the early morning,
Hoping it would last till you saw it.

It looks luvly, dunnit, said Margaret
(Christened Maggie) who cleans in the early morning.
I like to see it. Bud it means work.
Me 'usband's on't 'grittin, y'knaw.
'E were out last night from alf eight till eleven,
Then they gorrim up agen this mornin
At arf six. They do 't bus routes first.
On call they are, like. Y'can't gerraway of a weekend
From November till March. It's a responsibility.
Just Lancaster and Morecambe? Yeh. County
Does't motorway. They leave 't side roads
Till last. It's bus routes as cum first.
Taxed, they are, for overtime. I don't think it's fur.
Think of them electricians stuck on't mooer
Keepin power-lines clear. They get taxed for it.
Wheer should we be wi'out 'em?
They keep us all goin, like.

When I come back from talking to Margaret
(She doesn't like Maggie), your name was still there, Sophie,
But fading at the edges. I walked round it again.
Wake up quickly, before it goes.

In Memory

The florist is sympathetic. She chooses
Chrysanthemums of a subfusc tone,
Contributes a card: *with deepest sympathy.*

The undertaker is sympathetic. He
Bares respectful teeth, holding our sad
Flowers close to his expensive black bosom.

The city is not sympathetic. It is
Abstracted. In grassed-over graveyards
Pigeons and children gobble potato crisps.

From vicarages and surgeries, wherever
Sensitive celibate men resort,
Come sensitive celibate sighs of relief,

For you are dead, who pursued them with tiepins,
Cufflinks, tasteful Medici postcards,
And quietly intense conversation. You are

Dead, passed away in your sleep in your chaste bed-
Sitter with the charming rural views.
Tomorrow you will be incinerated,

Like the October leaves. Only leaves return
In a secure succession, and you
Leave just a few embarrassing ashes.

You have much to forgive us. Will you try? We
Are the acquaintances you wanted
As friends, friends who avoided proper passion,

Lovers who preferred the cordiality
Of friendship. Your embers reproach us.
Forgive us our fear, who need professionals

To love and mourn for us, who spread our futile
Euphemisms over suicide,
And ask for pardon from the careless dead.

What about Jerusalem?

'Would to God that all the Lord's people were prophets.' (*Numbers* 11;29)

Wallflowers in your garden are stubbornly rooted,
Heeled in by you. Your magnolia sprouts fierce black buds.

In Sheffield and Gloucestershire, babies you drew into light
Flower and grow upright A knack of giving life.

(I know 'em all, you'd swagger. *At least, their mothers I do.)*
They won't forget you, pain-killer, comforter.

Now you lie here in the chapel in pale wood,
White and yellow mortal flowers, and we sing

Jerusalem tentatively, waiting for you to pop up and exclaim
You've left out the feeling. So we have. I don't want to feel,

Gwen, that you've ended anything. *I will not cease*, we drone.
We haven't even started in the Great-heart way you did,

Who challenged geriatric consultants, hauled your friend
Out of dementia, brought her home to live.

Dear Gwen, who made the worst coffee I've ever tried
Not to drink, who never remembered a name

(You I mean! Whatnot!), who told explicit obstetric stories
Loudly, embarrassingly, in public rooms,

Who loved fast cars *(they pull in the birds)*
To my priggish disapproval; whose driving was known to the police.

I argued more with you than with anyone ever,
Though I'd seen you wink as you started to wind me up.

Is this all? Has that relentlessly
Self-educated mind at last run out of steam?

And such a little coffin. There's some trick here.
What about Jerusalem? You haven't ceased, have you?

A Wish for William Morris

(for Nick Bailey)

I'd have let him die here
That great lover of things
In the place he loved best.

Not graceless Hammersmith
That he healed in his book
But in the old manor,

Kelmscott by the river,
Where the bed was ready,
That he wrote the verse for,

May curtained, Jane sewed for,
With grass scent, late rose scent,
Invading the window,

Distant shouting of sheep,
A bravura blackbird,
Always his true love Thames.

The last time he came here
In springtime, in springtime,
Cuckoos whooped at seven,

Rooks and appleblossom,
Mediaeval garden,
Friend with a manuscript.

I'd have let him die then,
Saved from the wheelchair,
The hallucinations,

Blood leaping from his mouth,
Not knowing anyone.
He died in Hammersmith.

But they brought him home
In a harvest cart
Vine leaves all over

Past the house he'd found
To the church he'd saved
By his true love Thames.

O if there were justice they'd have saved him –
Twelve statues at Oxford on Mary Virgin's spire;
Blythburgh church; Peterborough's
Great interior; the north-west tower
At Chichester; the lock-keeper's roof
At Eaton Weir; a little barn
Vandalised at Black Bourton.

Fights of his last three years.

O if there were justice they'd have saved him –
The tower, the Suffolk angels, the non-pareil nave,
The tower, the roof, the barn – they'd have pulled him back
As he did them. And Rouen itself,
Rouen itself, and little Bourton
Would have come to deliver him.

But things are as they are.
It was raining. Leaves
Still on the lime-trees,
Church ready for harvest.

William Morris died at Hammersmith on 2 October 1896. His funeral took place on 6 October, at St George's Church, Kelmscott, Oxfordshire.

The Benefactors

They come provided with pins,
And buckets of cold water.

They never say *Well done!*
Or *We knew you could!*

They appear in the shape of the widow
Of a Scots GP. Mother has shunted you round

To announce you've won a college place,
First ever in the family.

You'd do better to stay at home, learning
To be the wife of some good man.

Or in the shape of a portly friend of your father's
Whom you overhear saying *Why waste money*

On educating a daughter? It's a poor investment.
You'll get nothing back.

        O thank you, benefactors,
Who said *Oh no!*

        You're making a big mistake.
Not at your age.

        What will the neighbours say?
You'll live to regret it.

        Not with the pound as it is.
I wouldn't if I were you.

Thank you for believing I couldn't do it.
Without your help, I'd never have brought it off.

Candidates should pay special attention...

Examiners' meeting near Christ Church, Bristol

Papers lie helpless on indifferent baize
By empty coffee cups and frayed cigars.
Here wait the awkward inarticulate
Statements of youth, complete with index number,
Headlong confidings of their shyest thoughts
On music, mothers, loneliness (the lines,
Like the punctuation, wobble with sincerity).

Attendant, too, articulated statements
On glossier paper, the poem, the slice of novel,
Exposed to be understood. Superior,
Correctly spelt, with an air of success about them,
Professional. But they are helpless too.
These hearts are pinned to paper, and are judged

By examiners. We sit here, and examine
Each others' accents and taste, and the wallpaper
(Emphatic for this room) and submissive scripts
For our prescribed two hours, while the wedding-party
In the next-door suite brawls on, and the quarter-boys
Of the neighbouring church divide our time between them.

We are examined too. Out standards vary,
We are moved by eloquence to ignore a faulty
Line of reasoning, or a misplaced comma,
Our marking will be marked, like the hotel walls,
The trusting candidates and the candid writers.
Only the flower-marked wedding guests are free
Of critical voices, though the well-fed speeches
Must be taxing somebody's patience this long afternoon,
And the boys on the clock have their measuring eyes on us all.

Lecture 1: Raising the Issues

At this stage you want to consider your assumptions.
Your Sixth Form teachers have probably taught you –
Can you read my writing from the back?
Can you hear me from the back?
Am I going too fast?

At this stage you want to consider. What kind
Of experience is going on there? (They are willing him
To say things they can write down, not to ask them questions.)
The kind of decision you have to make about this poem
Is: whether it really *works*. (Faces bend over paper
To avoid catching his eye.)

All right, let's move on. The sonnet
Is a structured emotion. The sonnet was,
For Elizabethans, a respectable type of form.
Here's just a little bit of historical background
Which hopefully will be useful to you: *Shakespeare
Changes the Focus of the Sonnet.*

Just to complete the circle, I hope you begin
To understand what you mean by poetry in general.
On your way out, please take a copy
Of the handout on Blake.

Seminar: Getting Worked Down

One day the Muse
Came to the Man
And charged him: Write!

Yeah, I jotted down a few ideas
(Says denim legs). We don't need
To read it aloud, do we? We've read it
Already, y'know. Well, if you say so

One day the Man
Finished the Work
And it was good.

How serious's it meant to be,
Like (asks Lancashire)? He doesn't seem to get
Worked up about anything much, does he? Keeps himself
From the run o'th' mill life, like.

One day the Judge
Admired the Work
And told the World.

Technique, yeah (says purple skirt).
Is it rhyming couplets when
Y'have drier and fire? I wouldn't
Have fancied being married to him at all.
Not a sort of happy chappie, is he?

One day the Board
Needing a Text
Picked out the Work.

I think he's having a good day
(Says acne man). There's that

Self-deprecating bit, yeah. But
S'more honest than the other ones, I think

> Students must read
> And Teachers study
> What the Board prescribes.

Can't say whether I like it
Or dislike it, really. Yeah, I like it.
He just doesn't want to get involved.
I don't like it at all.

> The Board, the World,
> Change Work to Text
> And gut the Man.

He's still alive?

Degree Day

Autumn brings them out of their
Pupation. They stand in the precincts, gowns
Fluttering in the approving air,
Still sticky from the chrysalis, unused
To wings and freedom. Their parents
Group round them, pleased but dubious,
Knowing they never got beyond
Caterpillars themselves, and wondering
If butterflies are better. Salad days.
Sunshine attached to the hoods
And gowns, inanely askew
In the modern wind. Has our breed always
Sported such fur, such brassy
Mediaeval colours? How will they cope
When it comes to finding a cabbage leaf
And settling down?

Now What?

I hereby release you from time;
From the tyranny of small comfortless rooms;
From crammed distressful lunch-breaks;
From coffee in paper cups. I divorce you
From the *you* that other people
Have decided you are; I restore to you
Sunday evenings. I have said
There shall be no more agendas;
No more reading of uncongenial papers
About quality control, accreditation, audit;
No more explaining the worth of unparalleled texts
To unimpressed note-takers. No more endless
Phone calls after midnight about
Abstracts, references, funding. No more
Paranoid colleagues, no more
Torpid secretaries. Finally
I invest you with the month of September,
Which you were last able to attend to
At the age of four. Hereby I give you
All this, said the magician. Freedom, it's called.

I thought you'd be pleased?

Pottery Class

They have all lived long enough to know better
Than hope, than children, or the doggedly
Recurring seasons.

Scuffed and weathered like old walls, grey-topped and quiet,
Sore from the banked-up troubles of a lifetime,
They are the clay, near clay, that shapes the clay.

At he end of illusion, you come to clay,
That yields and sulks and moves and thinks for itself
And is almost human,

That goes through fire, like us, and comes out better,
Handy about the house, the unassuming
Art of the scullery and the kitchen-garden.

The sorrowful man sees shapes in his dreams,
And waking shouts to the night *I could make that!*

Ben's Birthday

Some, before they learn to speak, can sing.

Entering the house, I heard the singer.
At ankle-height, he surfed, he chanted,
Raising his year-old face to smile
As each new friend came in.
                              O they were speakers,
All of them: Sonny who could stand,
Florence and James, the twins,
Curly-haired ginger grizzlers,
Brothers Thomas and Oliver,
Who kept together, cautiously, in case.

And the special one, Octavia,
Eight or nine years older than most;
Not as tall as all that, but wise,
Looking ahead, preventing collision,
Confusion, so young, so quick on the uptake
In the infantile hurly-burly. So unequivocally
Grown-up.

But the very special one, Ben,
The surfer, the ankle-height singer, the smiler
Who was friends with all.

                    This is for you, Samantha.
I saw it on his birthday, I wrote it for yours.

The Little Children and Their Wise Parents

(for Maisie Sanderson-Thwaite)

Sometimes grown-ups don't listen.
They hear what they think they hear.
Our parents are chuckling, and missing
The sadness of Mr Lear.

> He is very funny, our parents say,
> With his cat and his runcible spoons;
> Just the writer for you young shavers,
> With his drawings and words in festoons.

But can't you hear, O grown-ups wise,
That under the clowning he's crying?
That all his Jumblies have sailed away,
And Uncle Arly's dying?

> *Far and few, and they never came back,*
> *And we probably never shall see them more;*
> *They have sailed away, away, away*
> *To the Land of the Chankley Bore.*

Lionel worries about the Pobble,
Guy is sad about the Dong,
Violet weeps for the Yonghy-Bonghy-Bo.
Killing the rhinoceros was wrong.

> But he's really awf'ly funny, the grown-ups say,
> It's so pleasant to know Mr Lear,
> With Old Foss the cat, and his runcible hat –

> Violet's crying again. *O dear!*

Grandfather's Watch

Grandfather, with his Kaiser Bill moustache,
Who knows only the past and the present,
Trots in his ponytrap from patient to patient,
Charging the poor the least he can.

Tucked in his arm, by the waistcoat tick of his watch,
The child's too young to know who he is,
Nor does she know his enemies: TB, measles,
Pneumonia, the poor man's friend.

He'll never know the future, the National Health,
Antibiotics, sulphonamides, the transplant / bypass world
That she'll grow into. Heathrow, AIDS, computers.
His serious past her sepia history.

The great gold watch stays with her all the time.
Its florid initials. Its waistcoat tick,
Faithful and strong as it always was when he held it
In his helpless hands at the bedsides of the dying.

Wintersports

Winter is rook. He blunders stiffly
Down four hard months, darkness being
His mute barrage. Sometimes he over-reaches
Into powercuts, snow, fog. Then humanity,
Staging survival, the child's romp, swapping
Paraffin, antifreeze, anecdotes, becomes
Humane. Endless gentle erosion,
If only he knew, is his most mortal finesse.

The wretched are king; powerless,
And so beautiful. We revere them,
Comfort them with drugs, parlour games,
Short walks on sunny days, and are
At last checked by their endless
Vulnerability.

I endure winter, and the punctual
Attendance of the distressed
With the pawn's continuous midget acts
Of gallantry. But your absence is
Knight's move, the jagged cut
Clean across expectation.
I have no defence against it.

For Leo on 14.02.2000

Some whim of the calendar. For who
Could imagine the birds would woo
In mid-Feb, when we know quite well
That it's solstice-onwards that they do?

Some whim of the calendar. For who
But a martyr bishop that nobody knew
Would be linked with the business of kiss and tell
When a saucy young saintlet would do?

Ignoring the calendar, as I do,
Year in, year out, and leap-year too,
I may not love you especially well –
But I love you more dearly, I do.

All the same, I deplore the national neurosis
Which believes the best way to celebrate two hearts that beat as one is
A dozen long-stemmed martyred crimson roses.

Arthur's War

(for Maisie Hudson)

Always when it rains I think of Arthur,
Says Maisie, as the tourists huddle
Away from the brusque Venetian downpour
In expensive glittering arcades.
The rain saved his life in Italy,
Says Maisie, as the tourists finger
Curios, wondering who they'd do for.

Animal lover, a gentle man, our Arthur,
Says Maisie. Too imaginative for bayonet practice.
But there he was, in the army, fighting
His way up to Monte Cassino,
The big monastery. That's where he was shelled.
No, not dead. He was lucky. The Germans
Were bayonetting the injured on the ground.

So Arthur played dead. Lay on his face in the mud,
Says Maisie. Rain through his hair, down his legs all night
Till morning. Knew he mustn't move. And always
When it rains I think of Arthur, how the rain
Saved his life, and how he loathed it. Here
I am in Venice, and it's raining again. No,
Says Maisie, no more coffee, thanks.

Only four of them left at the end, only four,
Says Maisie. Arthur got a cushy number, after,
Guarding Italian POWs in Africa. *Bad soldiers,*
He'd say. *Just not good at fighting.* But clever
With their fingers, like the folk are here,
Says Maisie, glancing at the lustrous boutiques.
They were never idle, they'd make something from nothing,

Wood, cardboard, stones even. Whatever they made
Was fine. Arthur bought what he could. We have
Two boxes still, precious things, like in these shops.
He left them to me. That's why all this
Touches me. Reminds me of Arthur.

The filigree spoons. The elbowing crowds. The rain.

Road Rage on the M6

A killer, officer? Me? I know what I'm doing.
State of the art man, me. Look, I know this road
Like Eddie Stobart's lads, and Norbert Whatsit,
In fog, rain, cross-winds, junction to junction,
Honest-to-God professionals. It's the others –
Mobile phoners, lane-swoppers, old men in hats –
Shouldn't be allowed. So when this cretin
Creeps in at Cannock, cuts me up at Stoke,
I slammed him on the shoulder. Came at him.
He knew what I meant. Somebody had to tell him.
Somebody could've been killed, the way he was driving.

Libraries at War

The more you destroy them, the louder we call for books.
The war-weary read and read, fed by a *Library*
Service for Air-raid Shelters and Emergency Teams.

We can still come across them, the pinched economy
Utility war-time things, their coarse paper, their frail covers.
Such brightness in the dark: *Finnegan's Wake,*

The Grapes of Wrath, The Last Tycoon, Four Quartets,
Put out More Flags. On benches, underground,
In Plymouth, Southampton, Gateshead, Glasgow, in the Moscow Metro
They sit, wearing a scatter of clothing, caught off-guard,

The readers reading, needing it, while terror
Mobilizes in sound-waves overhead,
Lost in the latest. Something long. Or funny.

Fire, fear, dictators all have it in for books.
The more you destroy them, the louder we call.

When the last book's returned, there is nothing but the dark.

From the Captain's Log: An Alien in Residence

(for Tony Childs and Katherine Fanthorpe, who helped me to boldly go)

It had come to be a Resident, it said.
It arrived compatibly. We had just
Re-vitalised the primary sensors,
When it beamed up in the observation lounge,
Equipped with a name, a holograph, a protocol,
Utterly unfamiliar. Of course, we ran
A security diagnostic. It seemed OK.
Not a war-lord, certainly. Hadn't
A click of Klingon. Ears of
Humanoid texture, forehead no more corrugated
Than is commensurate with prolonged thought.
The Captain saw it as a malfunction
From the start. *Energy disruption field,*
He muttered. Also *Quantum singularity.*
Try another sensor reading.
      Sir! We snapped to it;
But all our serializations were identical.

It spoke our tongue. Shook hands with the Captain
(A social gaffe) and kissed Uhura (indelicate).
Produced documentation. Spoke of Arts,
And a Council (not known to our Federation),
Uttered in a pronounced anti-graviton layer.
Produced books (how did Galactic Customs let them through?)
Signed them; tried to sell them.

A hostile simulation programme (Doc's diagnosis).
It can't stay here, on the final frontier;
Using up words (and it's true,
It used a whole gravometric singularity
Of glossary, words like rhythm, rap, metaphor,

86

Irony, image, Shakespeare, none of which
We understood). *Energy relays are corroded,*
Says the engineer. *Affirmative,* says Captain.
All hands to psyonic resonators.
                          So we vaporised it,
Making ourselves safe to experience
Civilisation as we know it.

On the North Face

1975   Mr Wang (Chinese) meets Mr Hasegawa
Mr Wang has seen *a deceased person, an old body.*
English, English, he says. Next day
An avalanche kills him. Mr Hasegawa
Rue he should ask more detail.

Everest doesn't lose her dead. They sit upright,
Refrigerated, or lie as they fall, headlong,
Or choke in a crevasse. Few corpses
Break away from the mountain.

1924   Living, they went up the holy road,
Past the prayer stone beyond which
No life must be taken, to the wild North Face
Of the Goddess Mother, rock, snow, wind; implacable.

In tweeds, greatcoats, cardigans and scarves
They climbed, in home-knitted socks and hobnails.

1999   The Yanks who find him look like astronauts
In their correct kit. They're not prepared for this.
O my Gahd! O my Gahd! His matches.
His unpaid Gamages' bill. His letter from home
(The children have flu). He's one of them,

For all his old-world gear, his storm-bleached body.
This is Mallory. *A modern person.* A man they know.
We are disturbing him now.

His arm holds the mountain, won't let go.
They pray for him, sing a rather jaunty psalm.
Their awkward reverence needs other words:

O ye compassionate ones, defend Mallory,
Who is defenceless. Protect him
Who is unprotected. Who was last seen
Going strong for the top.

(*O ye compassionate*…Buddhist rite, from *The Tibetan Book of the Dead*)

Needle Work

I am the genius at the heart of things,
The answer at the middle of the maze,
Secret cartographer who tugs the strings,
The arrow that goes nowhere, but obeys
Earth's headstrong pull. North, south, east, west,
And all their subdivisions heed my mark;
The pioneers, the other-world-obsessed,
Follow from Erebus to Noah's Ark
My scarlet finger in the glassy box,
Directing humans through geography,
Through Roaring Forties to the fish-paved docks,
Through unmapped deserts to the tourists' sea.

But touch me not. Unless I'm free to roam,
You'll never set the course that brings you home.

Agnus Dei: 2001

When the days grow longer, they come,
White as newness. Life and soul
Of the flock, unlike their dingy elders.

In a good year, grow stockier,
Turn into sheep. In a bad year
Leave the world in summer, behind screens,

Smoke, silence, smell of disinfectant.

This one comes with the very early lambs
Always. Doing the things lambs do,
Lord of the dance in the meadow.

He knows where he's going.

Party Night

Busiest night of the year
Six-course corporate dinner,
Everything's gotta be OK –
Coffee, mints, walnuts, wine –
Wassail, as you might say.

Saw at once they had to go –
Not the party spirit.
Him, living on handouts, no doubt,
Her, in the family way. *No,* I said to the wife,
Not this night, of all nights.

Wife's obstinate. Typical.
Bedded 'em down in the shed, in the straw.
Quite envied 'em, rushed off me feet as I was,
Slaving over the wine and the women.

Missed what the wife says she saw –
Fireworks, singing, comets, royals.
Well, she may have. What I say is:
Who made the genuine profit that night?